TROUBLED LAND

TROUBLED LAND

THE SOCIAL LANDSCAPE OF NORTHERN IRELAND

PHOTOGRAPHS BY

PAUL GRAHAM

TEXTS BY

DECLAN McGONAGLE

GERRY BADGER

PUBLISHED BY

GREY EDITIONS, LONDON

WITH CORNERHOUSE PUBLICATIONS

TROUBLED LAND
Photographs by Paul Graham

ISBN 0 9508703 2 3

First Edition, 1987.
Photographs © Paul Graham, 1987
Foreword © Declan McGonagle, 1987
Afterword © Gerry Badger, 1987
Typeset by Artworkers, London EC1.
Printed by Jackson-Wilson, Leeds.
Published by Grey Editions,
14 Northwick House,
1 St John's Wood Road,
London NW8 8RD.

Publication subsidised by the
Arts Council of Great Britain.

TROUBLED LAND

NORTHERN IRELAND is a much photographed place. Certain perceptions of our situation are fixed. Sometimes it seems as if only certain perceptions are permissable (viz) tragic, turbulent, taciturn, tribal and tiresome. Confirming fictions is allowed but raising questions about understanding or even the desire to understand is not, as with the problem about screening the BBC's Real Lives programme 'At the Edge of the Union' in 1985. It's difficult even for people in Northern Ireland not to be conditioned by the pre-conditioned media.

Photography, as a cultural medium and one of the mass media has played an important role in documenting the current Troubles. In fact it defines as well as documents. The 'picturing' that has gone on has generally located the Troubles in one corner of a small island off Britain, off Europe. In reality the current Troubles are as old as this century, and not a single decade has passed during this when political conflict did not occur in Ireland. Historically our Troubles have been interwoven with the political, imperial, colonial ambitions and strategic interests of Britain and other European countries since before the reign of Elizabeth I. In one of Paul Graham's photographs children are seen playing in wasteground created by redevelopment in Belfast, beyond a pavement painted in fading red, white and blue. In the immediate foreground on the road, in front of a traffic ramp, is painted in orange the date 1690. What that refers to is the Battle of the Boyne, a crucial symbol of triumph for the loyalists of Northern Ireland, when King William of Orange defeated James II who was attempting to regain the English throne. In 1688/9 most of Ireland had declared for James II and it was only when earlier 'loyalists' besieged in the City of Derry for 105 days remained loyal to William that James' attempt weakened to be finally routed by William at the Boyne (a river North of Dublin) in 1690.

It is in the very ordinariness of this photographic image that lies its potential to illuminate by reflection. The 1690 refers to events 400 years old, yet the traffic ramp was put in place recently, at a time when this was an 'ordinary' street, to prevent one paramilitary group or another from speeding through such areas in cars, to carry out sectarian assassinations.

The past is right up against the present here. History has not been relegated to tourism. Issues are still current. We're still occupying the territory that was mapped out in 1690 and thereafter was overlain with myth. Ironically our 'marginal' legacy was created in the context of a conflict of European dimensions and importance (viz) the possession and succession to the English throne. Hence the durability of the political signs and slogans that pepper these photographs, drawn as they are from a well of historical meaning and reference which goes back centuries, yet are contemporary in their effect.

The Nationalist/Republican (IRA etc) and Unionist/Loyalist (UVF etc) signs are markers not only in the material, territorial sense but also of political possession and assertion. The accumulative effect of these images, their power, is to force a viewer to recognise that nothing is innocent, not even colours. Everything is emblematic. What is here in extremis in Northern Ireland, because it is the subject of the 'drama', is present if unrecognised in any state, any country. It's no surprise, but none the less shocking to see that prior to 1968 there was practically no mass media coverage of the political reality in Northern Ireland. It's to the eternal shame of an earlier generation of mediators in this society that it took the political violence of the late 60's and early 70's for lenses to be pointed in this direction: something which indicates a dominant attitude, (viz) an appetite for 'drama', against which Paul Graham's work stands in direct contrast.

In much of 'Troubled Land' it's as though he's not quite certain what he's found, unlike many photographers who have visited (Northern) Ireland only to find what they sought… who may have reacted against 'drama' only to look for and find the 'whimsical' or the 'primitive' – both marginalising qualities – who merely place themselves within set conventions of making photographic images. To some extent Paul has also worked within these

TROUBLED LAND

conventions only to emerge with a body of work that introduces the insecurity of questioning, his and our own questioning. In a cultural sense this places him and his work at the edge of the Union. To deal with this work is to deal with its subject.

Ireland was colonised and thereby marginalised by England. The Act of Union of 1800 destroyed Ireland's identity in the world as a nation State. In a sense England itself was colonised by a dominant class, but whereas the mechanics of domination in Ireland have remained visible because of the resistance, they have become invisible in what is now called mainland Britain. This is apparent in much work produced about Ireland, but is also present in work on aspects of life in Britain.

Since 1979 and the imposition of a particular type of conservatism whole areas of life, of experience, of identity have been similarly marginalised and devalued in Britain. Reaction to that marginalisation and the evaporation of confidence is growing, echoing the much longer process of denial and reaction in Ireland – denial in the sense that whole sections of the community were and are visibly denied access to power. The situation in Ireland, while compounded by the patina of tribalism and religion is deeply political and operates on exactly the same political principles as anywhere else, in relation to class and race. It is the drama of the Northern Irish situation that has got in the way and it is this drama that has been consistently projected, 'pictured' and in effect celebrated since 1968. If anyone comes to Paul Graham's 'Troubled Land' photographs expecting the vicarious excitement of that drama they won't find it, and it's to his credit that he doesn't set out to provide it.

A lot of cultural activity, a lot of Art and a lot of photography in particular, while aspiring to solidarity, actually contributes to this process of marginalisation by merely providing retinal reportage of the phenomena on the surface of the underlying political processes.

It is the absence of certainties that comes with reportage that makes 'Troubled Land' so unusual and refreshing. What Paul Graham is photographing is his own perplexity or incomprehenison at the sight of an armed soldier running for cover, for his life, in an 'ordinary' suburban street or the tattered Union Jack flag and election posters attached to trees in lush farmland which could pass for parts of England. For "parts of England" read normality,

> … when will we Germans be able to live normally,
> that is, forgetfully. (Gunter Grass)

The extraordinary regularly punctuates the ordinary in Northern Ireland, creating another type of reality which both sensitizes (signs and icons everywhere, in everything, to be subliminally read and understood) and de-sensitizes (alienation, brutality, desolation). It is this paradoxical reality which registers in Paul Graham's images.

Northern Ireland is a small place, geographically and psychologically, so it's virtually impossible to remain untouched by the Troubles or their effect. A vicious reality and pessimism are never far away, but when a society is in trouble, in a state of flux, then change is possible and optimism is essential. So while stagnant sectarian entrenchment looms on the one hand, the possibility of radical change is alive on the other. In 'Troubled Land' images which go beyond the superficial, the immediate or dramatic, are placed before people in Britain who need to see and understand them – a reversal of the colonial process.

The achievement of Paul Graham's photographs in 'Troubled Land' lies in providing a model for a new relationship, beyond political and cultural colonialism. Optimism is renewed.

Declan McGonagle,
Derry, 1987.

1: Union Jack Flag in Tree, County Tyrone, 1985.

2: Republican Parade, Strabane, 1986.

3: Turf Lodge, Belfast, 1984.

4: Shankill, Belfast, 1985.

5:    Graffiti on Phonebox, Belfast, 1985.

6:    Graffiti on Roadsign, Toome, 1984.

7:    Fading Political Posters, County Tyrone, 1985.

8:   Republican Posters, Gortin, County Tyrone, 1986.

9:   "1688 – 1690", Antrim, 1986.

10: Republican Housing Estate, Newry, 1984.

11:    Paint on Road, Gobnascale Estate, Derry, 1985.

13: Political Poster, Tate's Avenue, Belfast, 1985.

14:    Bombed RUC Station, Plumbridge, County Tyrone, 1986.

15: "IRA Lover", Ballysillan, Belfast, 1985.

16: Street Corner, Whiterock, Belfast, 1985.

17:    Newspaper Headline, Ardoyne, Belfast, 1986.

19:    H-Block Prison Protest, Newry, 1985.

20:    Republican Coloured Kerbstones, Crumlin Road, Belfast, 1984.

21:   Unionist Posters on Tree, County Tyrone, 1985.

22:     Army Helicopter and Observation Post, Border Area, County Armagh, 1986.

23:    Graffiti, Ballysillan Estate, Belfast, 1986.

24:    Army Stop and Search, Warrenpoint, 1986.

25:     Graffiti on Motorway Sign, Belfast, 1985.

26: Unionist Poster, County Antrim, 1985.

27:     "P.R.O.V.O.S." (Provisional IRA Graffiti), Newry, 1985.

28: Ardoyne Estate, Belfast, 1985.

29:   Unionist Coloured Kerbstones at Dusk, Near Omagh, 1985.

30:    "Eternity Where?", Ballymoney – Ballymena Road, County Antrim, 1985.

31: Cross Marking Site of Shooting, Shantallow Estate, Derry, 1985

TROUBLED LANDSCAPES

"What photographs of Ireland consistently fail to convey is the extent to which the landscape is constituted at the outset in social terms, whether as historical site, politically contested terrain, or as land and property. It does not lie beyond the domain of culture and politics but is firmly inscribed within it. The same applies to photographs of Northern Ireland which try to capture the 'normality' of everday life in the province as if some kind of privileged space lies beyond the political divide."

Luke Gibbons

WE SHOULD BEGIN BY considering the question of ambition in photography. For ambition, in what can be considered an assuredly positive manifestation, could be said to be one of the primary reference points for this work.

To many in the medium, ambition is synonymous with style. The height of ambition for most photographers is the attainment of a clearly recognised, acknowledged, individual 'style' – a visual signature. In essence, this might be described as a combination of two strategies, the marriage of a consistent choice of a strictly circumscribed subject matter with a consistently exercised schema of graphic construction. Reach this desirable state and the rewards can be considerable. The gaining of a 'name' and a readily saleable product – be the marketplace that of the magazine and art director, or the more rarified showcase of museum and curator.

However, there are photographers of a more serious and profound ambition, for whom the issue of style is secondary. Style is seen merely as the result of application rather than inspiration. For this minority, ambition extends beyond personal stylistic goals to the larger question of the medium's ambition. For them, that is a much more engaging, problematical, and ultimately challenging issue. What might photography, and photographers be? And crucially, what might they 'say'?

Until around a decade-and-a-half ago, the answer to that particular conundrum was relatively clear cut, and had remained so since the Nineteen Thirties. The few photographers of any serious ambition working in Great Britain between the Forties and the Sixties generally entertained two principal aims. Firstly, they desired to make cogently constructed, eloquent images in the manner of such mentors as Henri Cartier-Bresson or Bill Brandt. Secondly, they proposed to weave these singular images into a more complex and purposeful vehicle, a vehicle that might force a way beyond the medium's narrow, purely descriptive, non-narrative limitations. This vehicle became known as the 'picture essay'.

In short, the desired nirvana was art—journalism, a mode whereby the full potential of photography as a documentary art medium could be realised. The primary thrust of the medium was to be formalistic/sociological, the photographer to be a social artist who would construct a more or less narrative form in which photographs might make a 'creative', well intentioned comment upon society. The chosen vessel was to be the mass circulation magazine.

It is argued, with good reason, that this mode foundered upon its inherent inadequacies, those inadequacies perhaps ignored by its own hubris. One failing, undoubtedly, was that the ambitions of seriously aspiring photographers were curtailed drastically by the journalistic framework. The structure was too gargantuan, at once too inflexible yet too diffuse. It was too prone to compromise, functioning in the main as a series of controls in a scenario where photography inevitably was held to be subservient to the word. Although daily lip service was paid to the aphorism about a picture being worth a thousand words, in practice the word was held sacred, thus photographers' visions were diluted constantly by those who did not share their ambitions. Photographers seemed engaged in an endless war of attrition with those whose sympathies lay at the journalistic rather than the art

TROUBLED LANDSCAPES

end of the spectrum, and worse, who patently understood literary rather than visual qualities.

Nevertheless, perhaps more by accident than design and due largely to the inordinately obdurate efforts of a few rogue individuals, the system nourished some excellent photographers and generated some worthy work. It still flourishes, as inherently reactionary as ever, hardly changed except for an inevitable economic retrenchment in the face of television. As critic Rob Powell has written recently, the reportage mode is 'still the main theoretical foundation of the way the visual news media operate, or at least, are received throughout the Western world.' But the most ambitious photographers – excepting those whose ambitions lie in the direction of Messrs Porsche and Gucci – have left it far behind. The cutting edge of the medium lies elsewhere.

That cutting edge might be said to be a lot more oblique, and a good deal sharper than the relatively blunt instrument of classic reportage. Documentary realism could not be rationalised, packaged, and smoothed out so easily.

The most aware photographers began to realise this, as the burgeoning Seventies interest in photography – both as art form and as mass medium – released an unprecedented concentration of academic thinking upon the medium's aesthetic, sociological, political, and philosophical issues. The intriguing, nominally guileless little black box was rendered doubly fascinating in the light of its newly perceived lack of innocence, and the ever more complex questions of representation that it provoked.

It became apparent that the rather simplistic and often superficial tenets of the reportage mode no longer sufficed. the banalities engendered by the typical 'here today/gone tomorrow' assignment were obvious enough. (Five days in exotic location followed by glossy, 'in-depth' publication). Even if

wielded by more sophisticated hands and eyes, the credibility of the camera as any kind of authoritative witness could hardly be supported. Photographers simply had become much more aware of the medium's serious, probably fatal inadequacies in serving as direct explication for large events.

Paul Graham is one of a new generation of documentary/landscape photographers who eschew the conventional wisdom of photojournalism. His imagery is elliptical rather than direct, characterised by a plurality of concept that acknowledges the complex, slippery, wayward, ambiguous nature of the photographic medium. Like many of his contemporaries, such as Robert Adams, Chris Killip, John Davies, Lewis Baltz, or Martin Parr, his concerns are both social and formal. In a particular project, formal tendencies might appear to prevail over the social. In another, social meanings might dominate the formal. The general ambition, however, is to achieve a multi-levelled synthesis of cultural and formal meanings, within an overall rubric which may be described broadly as the workings of contemporary society – in one devious form or another.

Thus the old notion of the photographer as social artist still very much prevails. But the realisation that overt political statement in photography is at best a fugitive, uncertain goal, leads these photographers to tackle social themes and issues in a subtle, often oblique and inexplicit manner, concentrating upon what might be termed the subtext instead of the main plot. Their basic motivation is to make authentic, creatively valid comment, not propaganda. Formal, metaphorical, even playful opportunities are hardly denied, but actively pursued. Thus their work, though broadly socially oriented, is not political with a capital 'P'. The contemporary photographer of the 'social landscape' may be said to be more concerned with experience rather than history, with psychological rather than directly political states of being.

Such an approach, however, can unsettle those with a stricter ideological axe to grind. Graham's last book, 'Beyond Caring', consisted of colour photographs of the interiors of Social Security and Unemployment offices, seen from the customer's point of view. A sizeable minority of commentators accused the photographer of the heinous crime of formalism, and of presenting the work in an over-indulgent, art photographic style rather than the correct political context.

Perhaps some or these critics were unaware that a laminated, touring exhibition version of 'Beyond Caring' had been prepared to take the message to a non-'art circuit' audience. Or that the DHSS, unnerved by the garish colours and alienating soullessness depicted in the images, have instructed their interior design consultants to 'investigate'. Or even that the social implications of the book were discussed for ten minutes on the BBC's main radio lunchtime news. That, of course, has delighted the photographer – it is one test of whether his pictures touch the soul, of whether or not they are emotional and intellectual fakes. But part of their honesty, their authenticity is that element of formal play co-existing with the desperation. Graham was also delighted with his success in obtaining sharp, hand-held, medium format negatives in difficult conditions, and in creating a formal schema and a colour palette that reinforces the psychological experience his photographs are intended to convey.

'Authenticity' is a key word, it figures most highly amongst the ambitions of contemporary social landscapists, And authenticity, under such ambitious terms of reference, denotes sophistication, awareness, intelligence as well as simple integrity. It presumes a balanced awareness of the complexities of current imagistic issues. It might be equated, indeed, with non-superficiality, indicating a desire to push rigorously beyond the easy aspect and to ask more probing, often less finite questions. The photographer of true ambition holds the authentic in high esteem, and deprecates the superficial.

In this latest body of work, Graham's first ambition is to challenge what he perceives as the bland superficiality of our received photographic view of Northern Ireland. He is in agreement with a recent sentiment voiced by the Irish art critic, Brian McAvera:

> 'Living in Northern Ireland (or, I imagine, in any location which becomes a focus for the media) repeatedly reinforces an awareness of how photographic images simplify, distort, and devalue. An outsider, ignorant of the complexities of context, is encouraged to believe that comprehension can be equated with the striking image. Thus Belfast – or Beirut – becomes a hotspot notable for atrocity images.'

Therefore Graham –and in this he exhibits an article of faith that underpins not just his Irish project, but all his work – is directly challenging the reportage tradition, the tradition which nominally eschews 'formalism' in favour of 'content'. Yet its proponents collectively reduce content down to simplistic, formal metaphors. They have reduced the convoluted realities of Northern Ireland to one fundamental condition – mayhem. And note how the reduction becomes ever more intense (necessitating stronger doses of mayhem to touch us) as we fellow Brits – safely entrenched on *our* island – become increasingly inured to the whole business and thus diminish its newsworthiness.

Given that we on the mainland, or in Great Britain if you will, are fed a tightly controlled diet of news from Ulster – a thin, insubstantial diet, it might be said. Given that 'hard news' images and personality portraits are narrow, limiting areas. Beyond that, what do we have? We have a media that appears to have found the single, miracle image that says it 'all'. That image – we have all seen it – is the juxtaposition of the indigenous populace with the menacing/protective British peacekeeper/oppressor. This truly is the

TROUBLED LANDSCAPES

wonder image. For like many of the best cliches, it says all things to all people, and therefore has the priceless virtue of serving all sides in the propaganda sweepstakes. For the naively ambitious photojournalist, if the Brit is related visually to local children – innocence corrupted by experience and so on – the metaphors can get really heavy (handed).

There is another widely touted mode of Ulster imagery, the antidote to violence. It is incumbent upon the entrepreneurs, the Northern Ireland Tourist Board, and others with vested capitalist interests to counter the negative image of incessant strife. Persuade the visitor or potential investor that the Troubles are confined largely to a few working class ghettos inhabited by malcontents – now kept well under control. The remainder of the Six Counties is an unspoilt haven of misty green hills and charming, garrulous (of course simple) rustics – your John Coles and Frank Carsons rather than your Ian Paisleys or Gerry Adams'. As the man says, it certainly is the way you tell it.

All landscape bears the mark of economic, political and social as well as ecological forces. Many of these signs are discrete, largely subsumed into the fabric of the land, or else are so familiar that they go unheeded. But to an Englishman arriving in Northern Ireland, the ubiquity of the signs proclaiming tribal division, if not their overtness, effects a profound degree of culture shock. To be sure, the gable-end mural is as much a part of the North's iconography as the burning barricade, but the divisions are also celebrated – if that is the word – in a myriad of subtle ways, pervading 'normal' life in every sector of the community. There is, as Luke Gibbons writes, no privileged space beyond the conflict – contrary to the impression that the media and the Northern Ireland Office would seek to foster. The divisions are not localised, but permeate every aspect of life and work. You cannot escape to peaceful, natural green fields. Even a tree is partisan.

'Troubled Land' deals with the insistent signs of deep political division within the landscape. It is, therefore, inevitably concerned with boundaries, both tangible and ineffable. Boundaries between religions, ideologies, classes, histories, mythologies, peoples. The largest boundary, of course, unseen but looming over the work like the cranes at Harland and Wolff, is the boundary created when the Six Counties were forcibly wrenched away from the Irish Free State. The drawing of such expedient, divisive lines on the world map seems to have been an endemic feature of the British colonial enterprise. Divide and rule seems as much a product of British genius as the Industrial Revolution, and has left its own legacy of festering social spoil tips in return for short term pragmatism and an extra few decades exploitation of native resources.

The working class housing estates of Belfast and Derry look almost indistinguishable from their mainland counterparts in Liverpool and Glasgow. The fundamental circumstances of their residents' lives cannot differ all that much, except in one vital respect. They centre around the factory and dole office, the pub and bingo hall, the supermarket and the betting shop. Lives indelibly circumscribed by the strictures of class and hard economics.

But working class lives in Glasgow or Liverpool, deprived as they are, do not have to bear the unimaginable stresses and additional burdens imposed by history and perpetuated by vested political interests. Of course, with both cities linked so closely with Ireland, there is a degree of overspill from the Troubles which manifests itself on occasion, especially in dour, Calvinist Glasgow. But Catholic and Protestant live and work together. Job and housing discrimination on religious grounds is largely a thing of the past. (The evil having taken, it might be said, a recent racialist bias.) Only the frequent meetings of the local football clubs, particularly Rangers and Celtic in Glasgow, evoke the old enmities, now channelled relatively harmlessly into the ritualised warfare of sport.

Life in Ulster, however, is almost totally compartmentalised. Job discrimination (the last time there was a job) is a pernicious reality. And so the ritual signs of tribalism have proliferated. To paint, in normal circumstances, is a celebration, yet painting kerbstones in the sectarian colours of the North – red/white/blue, green/white/gold – seems more a final act of defiant despair. What could be a potential brightening up of a drab environment, serves only to place further boundaries around already circumscribed lives.

What usually is the 'normal' territorial imperative of disaffected adolescents, the spraying of gang slogans on telephone booths, an act of not-so-mindless vandalism, takes on specific and decidedly sinister overtones. The battle for supremacy on a phonebox is only a children's game, we might say, yet it reflects sectarianism in microcosm. The red 'UVA', oversprayed with 'IRA' in white, and then finally topped with a blue 'UVF'. These kids, once stained with their tribal colours, tainted with their mark, are unlikely to grow up and grow out of it.

Paul Graham's approach, as an Englishman intruding upon the Northern Irish scene – and he is very aware that he is an outsider – is to take a circumspect, ordered, and calmly distanced view. It might be said that such a role would be forced upon the lone English *flâneur* in Ulster, but Graham has chosen his ground quite deliberately. In this, he is in accord with much contemporary photography, where the approach might seem tentative, provisional, the grand gesture being eschewed in favour of a stance that is reticent, suggestive, cryptic, implicit. And, it should be noted, this work echoes the tenor of much recent Irish art, where, as Brian McAvera reminds us, 'shrewdness, ambiguity and the oblique approach are commonplace.'

Graham fully admits (as this writer would also admit) that he came to Northern Ireland with a degree of naivety. But to that word, with its perjorative connotation, let us add open mindedness and willingness to learn. I could not say lack of preconception, for of course we all have our preconceptions, formed by the photographs we have seen, but those preconceptions need not harden into pre-judgements.

The process of working for Graham, therefore, was a process of learning. His task, firstly, was to experience the situation at first hand, and then decide how he might convey the different texture of normality in the North to a largely non-Irish audience, without falling back upon the cliched excesses of much of the imagery he had viewed prior to his visits to the province.

Of course, although the primary ambition is to subvert the fragmentary and disassociated coverage of Northern Ireland, the work is itself only a fragment, a piece of the jigsaw. Nevertheless, in its openness, its lack of finiteness and certainty that might dismay some, there is an acknowledgement that the jigsaw exists. Photographs do not record 'whole' events, only fragments, often totally ambiguous and misleading fragments. The questions of reality versus fiction in a photograph, of media bias, and of truth versus propaganda, is a Gorgon Knot of fearsome complexity, but Graham has endeavoured to remain true to his experiences, to reflect if necessary an untidy, unfinished view. What has disappointed him has been the readiness of many relatively 'independent' photographers to take the easier option and fall back upon the superficial, cliched image.

One of the negative aspects of media coverage of the North is the tendency to artificially 'heighten reality,' by isolating any incident with a close-up. It is one of the sacred, unwritten commandments of reportage. 'If you're not in close enough, your pictures aren't good enough,' admonished Robert

TROUBLED LANDSCAPES

Capa, doyen of hotspot photographers. So *the* soldier is selected, *the* petrol bomb thrower is picked out, *the* bomb damage and only that shown.

Graham however steps back from the action, rather than stepping forward, to reveal what is above, below and alongside of it, integrating events into their surroundings. Overall, his intention is to develop a more reasoned and truthful balance between normality and conflict – a balance that perhaps might not pertain down the Falls Road, but was more indicative of the province generally.

We see, for example, a corniche road leading to an exemplary coastal village – an idyllic setting, a natural for the Irish Tourist Board. But the distant activity is a 'stop and search' operation by an army patrol. Crouched behind the sea wall is an observer, with binoculars firmly trained upon the suspicious figure of the photographer. The army's caution is understandable, and the ominous significance of this daily scene becomes clear when we learn that this quiet hamlet is Warrenpoint, in County Down, where eighteen British soldiers were killed by the IRA in August, 1979.

These photographs confound our expectations by pulling back and surprising us with the wider view. He reminds us that while the conflict's intrusion into everyday life is not as explosively evident as the media hype would have it, it nevertheless reaches far beyond the urban ghetto. Down an almost exaggeratedly lush, verdant country lane squats the ugly white shape of a fortified RUC station. Look more attentively and we notice the scars of a recent bomb attack. In another tourist board image *manqué*, we drive down a hill to a Derry sparkling in the distance, the sky filled with scudding white cotton wool clouds. But across the road surface, an unknown Unionist Jackson Pollack has flicked trails of red, white, and blue paint, sectarian blots on the landscape that – strangely – look as chilling as anything in 'Troubled Land' as they obscenely interrupt the idyll of the free, open road.

As typified by images such as the latter, Graham also plays with convention by working so blatantly in colour. That might not seem so unusual today. After all, many of the more ambitious contemporary photographers are utilising colour. (To the extent, perhaps, that the *really* ambitious are those who remain with black-and-white). However, the last media bastion of black-and-white, the one remaining area where the magazines and colour supplements still countenance black-and-white, is precisley where Graham has employed colour. Media black humour has it that, imagistically, the colour of blood is too bright, too upbeat to carry the full weight of an atrocity message. So the idiosyncracies of black-and-white are tolerated in the war zone, or social situations of comparable desperation – where the grittiest type of realism is called for. Thus the colour of the Ulster Troubles traditionally has been black-and-white.

To photograph in colour, therefore, is something of a heresy; and yet the grim, bright reality of Ulster lies in those three colour bands of green/white/gold and red/white/blue. The photographer aiming his camera at the social landscape of division could hardly avoid colour. And indeed, Graham, utilises it as effectively in Northern Ireland as he did in 'Beyond Caring' to reinforce his authenticity and slyly underpin his message.

'Troubled Land' should be viewed not simply in the context of Northern Ireland and its media coverage, against which it certainly is a reaction, but also in terms of current issues in advanced photography. There is, as I have indicated, a renewed focus upon social issues, though without the evangelical flavour of classic documentary and say, a W. Eugene Smith. And yet it ventures beyond the cynicism of the American documentary style of the late Sixties and early Seventies.

Amongst contemporary 'art documentary' photographers on both sides of the Atlantic, there seems an interesting, parallel mood of high seriousness, doom, and impending catastrophe. The Americans seem obsessed by the

TROUBLED LANDSCAPES

Apocalypse, whether man induced by nuclear means – Robert Adams, John Gossage, John Pfahl – or as the revenge of an imposed-upon ecology – Frank Gohlke, Emmet Gowin. Here in Britain, the mood is angrier, as photographers like Martin Parr, Chris Killip, Graham Smith, John Davies, and Paul Graham survey a more than potential breaking down of the fabric of British society.

Graham and his contemporaries are highly ambitious, in that they would have us read their photographs in ideographic terms, as representing ideas and not merely furnishing simple visual records or illustrations for words – the province mostly widely recognised hitherto for the medium. Their work, therefore, is difficult, dense, and often obtuse, requiring effort on the part of the viewer. Its natural forum is the book, where an extended dialogue can be set up – between image and image, between image and reader – and studied at leisure.

As a photographer of the social landscape, Paul Graham's ambition is to make resonant, oblique, layered statements, statements that assuredly are about the world, and human experience, but which also probe complexities of imagistic representation. The term 'landscape' itself incororates a dual notion. The idea of our environment as both a cultural and an imagistic construct, a wide-ranging, formal map of our experience patterns. Thus Graham is endeavouring not simply to record the external, material landscape in front of us, but also to reflect the inner model of the outer world, the social and cultural landscapes we use to organise our lives - and sadly, which in Northern Ireland we have used to destroy lives.

GERRY BADGER

COLOPHON

Paul Graham is an independent photographer living in London. He has exhibited widely across the U.K. as well as in America & Europe, and has had two previous books published: "Beyond Caring" which examines conditions in Welfare Offices across Britain, and "A1 – The Great North Road", a documentary on the nation's main North-South route. His photographs are in the collections of the Museum of Modern Art, New York, the Arts Council of Great Britain, the Victoria and Albert Museum and many others.

Declan McGonagle founded and ran the Orchard Gallery in Derry from 1978-84. He then worked as Director of Exhibitions at the Institute of Contemporary Arts in London until early 1986, when he returned to Derry to develop a series of new Arts Projects for the city council.

Gerry Badger is an architect who has been active as an image maker and writer since the early 1970's. His photographs have been widely exhibited, and he has been instrumental in organising several major exhibitions including "American Images", as well as being considered one of Britain's leading photography critics.

The photographs in this book were taken during 1984, 1985 and 1986 using a Plaubel Makina W67 Camera and colour negative film. The negatives were processed by LAB 120, 16 Blenheim Terrace, London NW8, and the photographs were processed entirely using May and Baker's "MYDOPRINT Professional" chemicals.

Thanks to Keith of Lab 120, Michael Arrowsmith of May and Baker, and Dewi Lewis of Cornerhouse.

Design: Paul Graham.
Typesetting: Artworkers, London EC1.
Printing: Jackson-Wilson Ltd, Leeds.

Photographs from this book can be bought from Grey Editions, 14 Northwick House, 1 St John's Wood Road, London NW8 8RD, England.

This book was supported by a generous publications grant from the Arts Council of Great Britain.